The MARVELous
STAN LEE

The MARVELous
STAN LEE
By EllenAim

FILM STARS
Volume 3

Creative Media Publishing

CREATIVE MEDIA, INC.
PO Box 6270
Whittier, California 90609-6270
United States of America

The scanning, uploading, and distribution of this book via the Internet or via any other means without the permission of the publisher is illegal and punishable by law. Please purchase only authorized electronic editions and do not participate in or encourage electronic piracy of copyrighted materials. Your support of the authors' rights is appreciated.

The publisher does not have any control and does not assume any responsibility for author or third-party website or their content.

Book & cover design by Joseph Dzidrums

www.creativemedia.net

Copyright © 2017 by Creative Media, Inc. All rights reserved.
Printed in the United States of America.

First Edition: May 2017

LCCN: On File
ISBN 978-1-938438-52-3
eISBN: 978-1-938438-53-0

To Cody

TABLE OF CONTENTS

Chapter One
Ravenous Young Reader — 9

Chapter Two
A Timely Job — 15

Chapter Three
A New Type of Comic — 25

Chapter Four
Legend — 33

Quotes about Stan Lee — 45

Movies Based on Marvel Comics — 46

Television Based on Marvel Comics
Live Action — 48

Television Based on Marvel Comics
Animated — 49

Essential Links — 50

About the Publisher — 51

Chapter One
Ravenous Young Reader

"Every day is a new adventure."

On a cold day on December 28, 1922, Stanley Martin Lieber was born in Manhattan, New York. His parents were Jack and Celia, two immigrants from Romania, a country in Southeastern Europe. Today, most American babies enter the world in a hospital, but Stan arrived in his mother and father's apartment at the corner of West 98th Street and West End Avenue.

Stan's parents struggled with finances while they were raising him. His father, a skilled dress cutter, often had difficulty finding work during the Great Depression, a time of economic disaster during the 1930s which saw many people unemployed, hungry, and homeless.

When Stan was eight years old, his brother, Larry, was born. Because of their vast age difference, the siblings weren't tight as children, but they grew closer later in their lives.

The MARVELous Stan Lee

By Ellen **Aim**

In their early years, the brothers shared a room in the family's one-bedroom Bronx apartment. Meanwhile, their parents slept on a pull-out sofa in the living room. Stan felt disappointed that their residence's lone window faced a brick wall, and he vowed to rent an apartment one day that overlooked the street.

When Stan reached his teenage years, he had developed a passion for reading and writing. The enthusiastic reader loved *The Hardy Boys*, a book series about teenage brothers who solve mysteries.

"One of the best gifts I ever got — [my mom] bought me a little stand that I could keep on the table while I was eating, and I could put a book on the stand, and I could read while I was eating," he told *NPR*. "I mean, I always had to be reading something."

In fact, Stan adored great stories in general. On weekends, he walked to a Loews movie theater near his apartment to catch a discount matinee. He loved that the movie house featured a live organist who played tunes before each showing. The film buff felt especially excited when a movie would star his favorite actor, swashbuckler Errol Flynn.

"I would leave the theater," he told *CBS News*. "I had an imaginary sword at my side, and I'd be looking for some girl that some bully was picking on so I could run to her rescue."

During the day, Stan attended classes at DeWitt

Clinton High School, a public, all-boys institution in the Bronx. He graduated with the class of 1939 at the age of 16. The youngster finished school early because he wanted to get a job and contribute financially to his family.

Throughout his school years, Stan had juggled several part-time jobs. He flexed his writing talents by penning obituaries for a news service and wrote press releases for the National Tuberculosis Center. The earnest teen also earned money by delivering sandwiches, working as an office boy, ushering at a movie theater, and selling subscriptions for the *New York Herald Tribune* newspaper.

Little did he know that his first full-time job would change his life and forever alter the comic book universe.

ʙʏEllen**Aim**

Errol Flynn's Hollywood Walk of Fame Star
Joseph Dzidrums

CHAPTER TWO
A Timely Job

"In the days that I was writing those stories, I just hoped that the books would sell and I'd be able to get my salary and pay my rent."

In 1939, Stan's uncle, Robbie Solomon, helped him land a job at Timely Comics, the comic book branch owned by American publisher Martin Goodman. Every weekday, Stan entered the McGraw-Hill Building on West 42nd Street to work as an assistant. His responsibilities included filling inkwells, fetching coworker's lunches, and sometimes proofreading books.

Timely's main competitor at the time? DC Comics. They published such famous comic books like *Superman*, *Batman*, and *Green Lantern*.

DC Comics didn't impress Stan. One of his biggest issues with their books? He disliked their stories' vague settings.

"I didn't enjoy stories that took place in a Gotham or Metropolis," he told the *Chicago Tribune*. "I didn't know where those places were! Why couldn't it be a New York, Chicago, Los Angeles?"

Meanwhile, Timely Comics had a well-known fictional character named Captain America. Created in early 1941, the patriotic hero with superhuman abilities, thanks to an experimental serum, fought the Axis powers led by Nazi Germany during World War II. Readers loved the brainy, brave superhero and eagerly anticipated his new adventures.

"My theory about why people like superheroes is that when we were kids, we all loved to read fairy tales," he later told *The Washington Post*. "Fairy tales are all about things bigger than life: giants, witches, trolls, dinosaurs and dragons and all sorts of imaginative things. Then you get a little bit older, and you stop reading fairy tales, but you don't ever outgrow your love of them."

Stan was a hard worker who could churn out copy quickly. He also possessed enormous confidence and a fervent desire to learn every facet of the comic book industry. His admirable qualities made him an asset at Timely Comics, and the poised young man catapulted up the ranks at the publishing company.

In spring of 1941, Stan had his first work published in the comic book *Captain America*. His text filler, a two-page story without illustrations, appeared in the issue entitled "Captain America Foils the Traitor's Revenge." The teenager adopted the pseudonym Stan Lee for the piece because the aspiring author wanted to save his real name for a novel that he hoped to someday pen.

Several months later, Stan had the opportunity to write an actual comic with the backup feature "Headline' Hunter, Foreign Correspondent." The writer also conceived the new creations, Jack Frost and Father Time.

In late 1941, following a dispute with Goodman, editor Joe Simon, and his creative partner Jack Kirby resigned from Timely Comics to work for a competitor named National Comics. Due to the publishing company's shakeup, eighteen-year-old Stan became the interim editor. The young man seized the opportunity and flourished in his new role. As a reward, he won the position permanently.

In 1942, Stan Lee enlisted in the U.S. Army because he felt determined to do his part during World War II. The American initially served in the Signal Corps and spent his time repairing communications equipment. Later, his superiors relocated him to the Training Film Department, His official position? Playwright. He wrote writing manuals, training films, slogans, and even occasionally drew cartoon posters.

Because Stan was a skilled writer who produced work quickly, he frequently had ample spare time. As a result, he began doing freelance work for Timely Comics. He often wrote copy and mailed it to the publishing company.

Eventually, Stan received a transfer to Duke

University. During this time, he purchased his first automobile, a 1936 black Plymouth with white tires and red seats. The car enthusiast paid twenty dollars for the third-hand vehicle and proudly drove it anytime he could.

In 1945, Stan returned home to New York and resumed his job at Timely, which became Atlas Comics several years later. For a while, he wrote a broad range of stories covering many genres, like westerns, romance, humor, science fiction, and horror.

Ever since Stan was a boy, he had drawn pictures of his idea of the world's most beautiful woman. In 1947, Stan agreed to a blind date with a model named Betty. When he arrived at her apartment to meet her, her friend, a gorgeous redhead named Joan Clayton

Boocock, answered the door instead. The smitten man couldn't believe his eyes. The ideal woman that he had drawn so many times over the years stood before him.

"May I help you?" she asked in a beautiful British accent.

The enamored man blurted out, "I love you."

Stan had just met his dream woman, and Joan considered him the best-looking man she had ever seen. The smitten pair went to lunch together and learned they had much in common. They married a few weeks later on December 5, nearly two weeks before the groom's 25th birthday. He later described his wedding as the greatest birthday gift ever.

Five years after marrying, Stan and Joan welcomed a daughter into their lives. Joan Celia Lee was born on January 1, 1950. Sadly, the couple's second daughter, Jan, died shortly after her birth.

After the death of their second child, the Lees briefly considered adopting another child but ultimately abandoned the plans.

One child was enough for them.

Stan enjoyed being a father to Joan Celia, or J.C., as her parents called her. He frequently spent afternoons playing with his daughter and their two German Shepherds, Blackie and Simba.

Near the end of the 1950s, Stan had grown increasingly discontented with his career. He wasn't enjoying working in the comic book industry anymore and told his wife that he might quit the business. Joan suggested that before her husband resigned, he should create a story that he had always wanted to write but hadn't done.

Stan respected his wife greatly and took her suggestion to write for himself. So, he created a story about a group of superheroes who grappled with a flawed humanity. He called his work *The Fantastic Four*.

Chapter Three
A New Type of Comic

"I always wrote for myself. I figured I'm not that different from other people. If there's a story I like a lot, there's got to be others with similar tastes."

In November of 1961, *The Fantastic Four*'s first issue hit newsstands under Timely's new name Marvel Comics. For only ten cents, readers delved into the 25-page story of four superhero friends who acquired their powers after being exposed to cosmic rays during an outer-space assignment.

"I hate to sound immodest, but with *The Fantastic Four*, I started a new type of comic," Stan told *Men's Journal*. "I tried to give the characters their own personality and their own problems and way of talking and acting. That hadn't been done in comics before, and the book did very well."

The Fantastic Four, created by Stan and Jack Kirby, became an instant success. Feeling reignited by the series' popularity, Stan remained with Marvel Comics. He felt a burst of inspiration for a whole new crop of stories.

In August of 1962, with artist Steve Ditko, Stan created his most famous character ever: Spider-Man. High school student Peter Parker, an orphan raised by his Aunt May and Uncle Ben, who gains super strength and spider-like abilities when a radioactive arachnid bites him.

"I saw a fly crawling on a wall, and I thought, 'Gee, what if a guy could stick to walls like an insect?'" Stan told *CBS News*. "That sounds good. So I started trying to think of some names. Insect-man? Nah.

Mosquito-man? Nah. And then I got to *Spider-Man*. Spider-Man, ooh, that sounds dramatic! And if he has spider power, he can shoot a web also. And he could swing!"

Spider-Man became Marvel's best-selling comic. An instant pop icon, the character developed a large, devoted audience among college students. Shortly afterward, it inspired a self-titled animated series. By the 1970s, the superhero also headlined two comic books. He also appeared on pinball machines, novels, t-shirts, action figures, rings, belt buckles, watches, pens, mugs, and more.

"I wanted [Peter Parker] to look like a typical, thin high school kid," Stan told *NPR*. "And he doesn't get all the girls because of his athletic prowess. He's just kind of a shy high school kid who's a science major."

The Hulk, inspired by *Frankenstein* and *Dr. Jekyll and Mr. Hyde*, premiered in the same year as *Spider-Man*. After being exposed to gamma rays, a socially awkward physicist becomes physically transformed into the burly, green-skinned, anger-ridden Hulk whenever he endures stress.

By the 1970s, the green monster was seen weekly on CBS's television drama *The Incredible Hulk*. The popular live-action series starred Bill Bixby as David (changed from Bruce) Banner and professional bodybuilder Lou Ferrigno as Hulk. Over the show's four-year run, it received three Primetime Emmy nominations, including Mariette Hartley's win for Outstanding Lead Actress in a Drama Series for her portrayal of Dr. Carolyn Fields, Banner's doomed fiancée.

Bill Bixby & Lou Ferrigno in THE INCREDIBLE HULK

The Incredible Hulk ran for five straight seasons. Stan and Jack made cameo appearances in the series, while it assembled a lengthy list of well-known guest stars over the years, like Kim Cattrall, Ray Walston, Rick Springfield, and Loni Anderson. Following the show's cancellation, NBC aired three Hulk television movies starring Bixby and Ferrigno.

Meanwhile, Marvel Comics produced other successful characters as well. Stan helped create characters like Iron Man, Thor, and Doctor Strange. The comics were all big successes with enthusiastic fan bases.

In September of 1963, the *X-Men* comic book series premiered. Created by Stan and co-writer/artist Jack Kirby, a group of mutant superheroes with superhuman strengths fought for peace and equality in a world saddled with prevalent anti-mutant bigotry.

"It was an anti-bigotry story," Stan told *Bloomberg.com*. "People hated and feared the X-Men because they were different. And I wanted to show that everybody is different in some way or other, and it's wrong to hate somebody because of the difference."

By the early 1970s, Stan stopped writing comic books to assume a new role. He became Marvel's publisher. Additionally, the highly-respected man watched his popularity rise while making numerous public appearances. The amiable storyteller frequently hosted question & answer sessions on college campuses and at comic book conventions. Before long, Stan Lee and Marvel became synonymous with one another.

Chapter Four
Legend

"I love working on stories, and luckily that's the one thing that age doesn't really stop you. You don't have to be incredibly powerful like the Hulk in order to dream up stories."

In 1981, Stan and Joan made a momentous personal decision when the happy couple moved to sunny Southern California. The Lees adored New York, but they grew to love their new home, too. The state's warm weather, vibrant trees, and bountiful movie studios appealed greatly to them.

On July 12, 2000, 20th Century Fox released the live-action *X-Men* movie. Directed by Bryan Singer, the film starred Hugh Jackman, Patrick Stewart, Halle Berry, and Ian McKellen. The slick vehicle earned high marks from movie critics and moviegoers. It grossed over $54 million dollars in its opening weekend, a record at the time for a comic book adaptation.

Stan felt tickled when producers asked him to make a cameo appearance in *X-Men*. The man who entertained acting dreams in his youth appeared in the movie as a hot dog stand vendor on the beach when Senator Kelly emerges from the ocean.

On May 3, 2002, Columbia Pictures released the long-awaited *Spider-Man* movie. Directed by Sam Raimi, the film starred Tobey Maguire as Peter Parker/Spider-Man, Kirsten Dunst as Mary Jane Watson, Willem Dafoe as the Green Goblin, and James Franco as Harry Osborn. Critics enthusiastically embraced the movie, and moviegoers helped it gross over 100 million dollars in its opening weekend, the first film to accomplish that feat. Two sequels and a pair of reboots followed *Spider-Man*.

Iron Man Suit Display
bedobedo

By the 21st century, Marvel was more popular than ever. Throughout the years, Hollywood repeatedly looked to the company for film material. *Hulk, Iron Man, Thor, Daredevil, Captain America, The Avengers, Ant-Man, Doctor Strange,* and *Guardians of the Galaxy* all received big-screen treatments.

2012 DragonCon Parade
RobHainer

"When I watch these movies, I watch them just as any fan," Stan told *Esquire*.

Television also hopped on the Marvel craze. *Agents of S.H.I.E.L.D* and *Agent Carter* joined ABC's broadcast lineup. Meanwhile, Netflix gobbled up Marvel properties by airing numerous comic book TV series: *Jessica Jones, Daredevil, Luke Cage, Iron Fist, The Defenders,* and *The Punisher*.

Stan & Actress Scarlett Johansson at THE AVENGERS Los Angeles Premiere
Jean_Nelson

On August 31, 2009, Disney announced that they would purchase Marvel for $4 billion dollars. The family-oriented corporation felt pleased with the deal. The publishing company's literary properties appealed to young boys; a demographic Disney hoped to strengthen.

Disney Chief Executive Robert Iger told *CNNMoney.com*, "This treasure trove of over 5,000 characters offers Disney the ability to do what we do best."

In 2010, Stan created the Stan Lee Foundation. The American non-profit organization sought to create access to literacy, education, and the arts. The project felt near to the writer's heart.

J.C., Stan, and Joan at DVD Exclusive Awards
s_buckley

"I started the Stan Lee Foundation for one main purpose: to do whatever I could to fight illiteracy in children," he explained to *The Washington Post*. "The ability to read well, to study, comprehend, and process information is absolutely vital for success as an adult."

Over the years, Stan racked up several appearances in various Marvel films. For years, fans speculated that Stan was playing the same character in all his cameos. They believed he was Uatu, also known as The Watcher, a fictional character that appears in Marvel's comic books

When rumors wouldn't die, Marvel had a little fun with them. In 2017's, *Guardians of the Galaxy Vol. 2*, Stan's cameo involved him sitting talking with other Watchers.

"We thought it would be fun to put that in there because that really says, so wait a minute, he's this same character who's popped up in all these films," Marvel Studios boss Kevin Feige finally commented on them.

A common question that people often asked Stan Lee? Who was his favorite comic book character? The writer could never choose one; he loved them all. When asked which superhero he wanted to be, Stan offered a witty response.

"I'd like to have Tony Stark's money and charm and irresistibility," he revealed to *Forbes*. "I would like to have Spider-Man's ability to swing through the city. I would like to be able to go up to Asgard, like Thor, and consult with the gods. I wish I were as strong as the Hulk. Every one of them has something good about them."

Throughout Marvel's huge success, Stan enjoyed being the face of the brand. The magnetic personality visited talk shows, podcasts, and appeared on guest panels to discuss his beloved characters. He also kept busy with his production company, Pow Entertainment. Always a hard worker, he was discontent to rest on his laurels.

"Y'know, most people, when they retire, they say, 'At last, I'll have a chance to do what I've always wanted to do,'" Stan told *CNN*. "But I'm doing what I've always wanted to do! I'm working with artists, writers, with directors. I'm working on creative things. I'm having fun! I mean, don't punish me by making me retire."

Stan Lee at the THOR Los Angeles Premiere
PopularImages

THOR: THE DARK WORLD Los Angeles Premiere
s_bukley

Joan and Stan at Covenant with Youth Gala
s_bukley

Stan & Joan at the 2011 Hollywood Walk of Fame Induction
s_bukley

QUOTES ABOUT STAN LEE

"His name is the first name you think of when you think of Marvel."
Actor Clark Gregg

"He created characters who were so incredibly out of the box and so inventive that, as a child, you were enthralled."
Actor Theo Rossi

"He can recite anything by Shakespeare, by Rudyard Kipling, I mean, he's really a man of the word."
Daughter J.C. Lee

"If Stan hadn't been doing those stories that were for teenagers and not kids, comics would have disappeared."
Tom Spurgeon, Biographer

MOVIES BASED ON MARVEL COMICS

Captain Marvel	Fantastic Four
1944	2005
Howard the Duck	X-Men: The Last Stand
1986	2006
The Punisher	Ghost Rider
1989	2007
Captain America	Spider-Man 3
1990	2007
The Fantastic Four	Fantastic Four: Rise of the Silver Surfer
1994	2007
Blade	Iron Man
1998	2008
X-Men	The Incredible Hulk
2000	2008
Blade II	Punisher: War Zone
2002	2008
Spider-Man	X-Men Origins: Wolverine
2002	2009
X2	Iron Man 2
2003	2010
Hulk	Thor
2003	2011
The Punisher	X-Men: First Class
2004	2011
Spider-Man 2	Captain America: The First Avenger
2004	2011
Blade: Trinity	Ghost Rider: Spirit of Vengeance
2004	2012
Elektra	The Avengers
2005	2012

MOVIES BASED ON MARVEL COMICS

The Amazing Spider-Man	Doctor Strange
2012	2016
Iron Man 3	Guardians of the Galaxy Vol. 2
2013	2017
The Wolverine	Spider-Man: Homecoming
2013	2017
Thor: The Dark World	Thor: Ragnarok
2013	2017
Captain America: The Winter Soldier	Black Panther
2014	2018
The Amazing Spider-Man 2	New Mutants
2014	2018
X-Men: Days of Future Past	Avengers: Infinity War
2014	2018
Guardians of the Galaxy	Deadpool 2
2014	2018
Avengers: Age of Ultron	Ant-Man and the Wasp
2015	2018
Ant-Man	Dark Phoenix
2015	2018
Fantastic Four	Venom
2015	2018
Deadpool	Captain Marvel
2016	2019
Captain America: Civil War	Spider-Man: Homecoming 2
2016	2019
X-Men: Apocalypse	
2016	

TELEVISION BASED ON MARVEL COMICS
Live Action

Spidey Super Stories *1974–77*	**Luke Cage** *2016–present*
The Amazing Spider-Man *1977–79*	**Legion** *2017–present*
The Incredible Hulk *1977–82*	**Iron Fist** *2017–present*
Spider-Man *1978–79*	**The Defenders** *2017*
Mutant X *2001–04*	**The Punisher** *2017*
Blade: The Series *2006*	**Inhumans** *2017*
Agent Carter *2015–16*	**The Gifted** *2017*
Agents of S.H.I.E.L.D. *2013–present*	**Cloak & Dagger** *2018*
Daredevil *2015–present*	**New Warriors** *2018*
Jessica Jones *2015–present*	**Runaways** *2018*

TELEVISION BASED ON MARVEL COMICS
Animated

The Marvel Super Heroes *1966*	The Avengers: United They Stand *1999–2000*
Fantastic Four *1967–1968*	X-Men: Evolution *2000–2003*
Spider-Man *1967–1970*	Spider-Man: The New Animated Series *2003*
The New Fantastic Four *1978*	Fantastic Four: World's Greatest Heroes *2006–2007*
Fred and Barney Meet The Thing *1979*	The Spectacular Spider-Man *2008–2009*
Spider-Woman *1979–1980*	Wolverine and the X-Men *2008–2009*
Spider-Man *1981–1982*	Iron Man: Armored Adventures *2009–2012*
Spider-Man and His Amazing Friends *1981–1983*	The Super Hero Squad Show *2009–2011*
The Incredible Hulk *1982–1983*	The Avengers: Earth's Mightiest Heroes *2010–2013*
X-Men *1992–1997*	Marvel Anime *2011–2012 (U.S.)*
Fantastic Four *1994–1996*	Ultimate Spider-Man *2012–2017*
Iron Man *1994–1996*	Hulk and the Agents of S.M.A.S.H. *2013–2015*
Spider-Man *1994–1998*	Marvel Disk Wars: The Avengers *2014–2015 (Japan)*
The Incredible Hulk *1996–1997*	Avengers Assemble *2013–present*
Silver Surfer *1998*	Guardians of the Galaxy *2015–present*
Spider-Man Unlimited *1999–2001*	

Essential Links

Official Websites
www.stanleestuff.com

Pow Entertainment Official Website
www.powentertainment.com

Twitter
@TheRealStanLee

Instagram
www.instagram.com/therealstanlee

ABOUT THE PUBLISHER

Creative Media Publishing has produced biographies on several inspiring personalities: *Simone Biles, Nadia Comaneci, Clayton Kershaw, Mike Trout, Yuna Kim, Shawn Johnson, Nastia Liukin, The Fierce Five, Gabby Douglas, Sutton Foster, Kelly Clarkson, Idina Menzel, Missy Franklin* and more. They've published two award-winning Young Adult novels, *Cutters Don't Cry* (Moonbeam Children's Book Award) and *Kaylee: The "What If?" Game* (Children's Literary Classic Awards). They have also produced a line of popular children's book series, including *The Creeper and the Cat, Future Presidents Club, Princess Dessabelle* and *Quinn: The Ballerina*.

www.CreativeMedia.net
@CMIPublishing

FILMSTARS™
Hollywood's Brightest

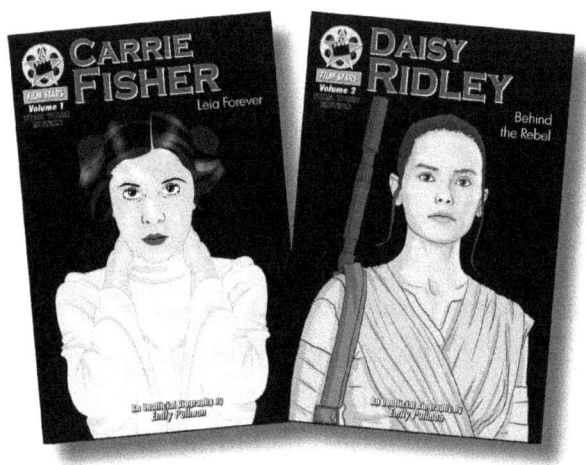

Before she was **Princess Leia** in *Star Wars*, **Carrie Fisher** was a young girl who loved to read and write and just happened to have famous parents. She never dreamed of being an actress like her mother, **Debbie Reynolds**, or a singer like her father, **Eddie Fisher**. When she auditioned for a sci-fi film on a whim, she had no idea it would change her life and turn her into a film icon. *Carrie Fisher: Leia Forever* is a biography for young readers who want to know more about the woman behind **Princess Leia**.

BUILD YOUR GYMNSTARS™
Collection Today!

Now sports fans can learn about gymnastics' greatest stars! Americans **Shawn Johnson** and **Nastia Liukin** became the darlings of the 2008 Beijing Olympics when the fearless gymnasts collected 9 medals between them. Four years later at the 2012 London Olympics, America's **Fab Five** claimed gold in the team competition. A few days later, **Gabby Douglas** added another gold medal to her collection when she became the fourth American woman in history to win the Olympic all-around title. The *GymnStars* series reveals these gymnasts' long, arduous path to Olympic glory. *Gabby Douglas: Golden Smile, Golden Triumph* received a **2012 Moonbeam Children's Book Award**.

Y Not Girl™
Women Who Inspire!

Our **YNot Girl** series chronicles the lives and careers of the world's most famous role models. ***Jennie Finch: Softball Superstar*** details the California native's journey from a shy youngster to softball's most famous face. In ***Kelly Clarkson: Behind Her Hazel Eyes***, young readers will find inspiration reading about the superstar's rise from a broke waitress with big dreams to becoming one of the recording industry's top musical acts. ***Missy Franklin: Swimming Sensation*** narrates the Colorado native's transformation from a talented swimming toddler to queen of the pool.

STAGESTARS™
Broadway's Best!

After her triumphant turn as *Thoroughly Modern Millie*, Sutton Foster charmed Broadway audiences by playing a writer, a princess, a movie star, a nightclub singer, and a Transylvania farm girl. A children's biography, **Sutton Foster: Broadway Sweetheart, TV Bunhead** details the role model's rise from a tiny ballerina to the toast of Broadway.

Idina Menzel's career has been "Defying Gravity" for years! With starring roles in *Wicked* and *Rent*, the Tony-winner filmed a recurring role on *Glee* and lent her talents to the Disney films, *Enchanted* and *Frozen*. A children's biography, **Idina Menzel: Broadway Superstar** narrates the actress' rise to fame!

Get ready to chase your dreams after reading this thrilling children's biography on *Hamilton* creator **Lin-Manuel Miranda**. A terrific source for a book report, **Lin-Manuel Miranda: Lights Up** tells the inspiring life story of the role model's transformation from a young boy with Broadway dreams to one of today's most respected artists.

FAIR YOUTH
Emylee of Forest Springs

Twelve-year-old Emylee Markette has felt invisible her entire life. Then one fateful afternoon, three beautiful sisters arrive in her sleepy New England town and instantly become the most popular girls at Forest Springs Middle School. To everyone's surprise, the Fay sisters befriend Emylee and welcome her into their close-knit circle. Before long, the shy loner finds herself running with the cool crowd, joining the track team and even becoming friends with her lifelong crush.

Through it all, though, Emylee's weighed down by nagging suspicions. Why were the Fay sisters so anxious to befriend her? How do they know some of her inner thoughts? What do they truly want from her?

When Emylee eventually discovers that her new friends are secretly fairies, she finds her life turned upside down yet again and must make some life-changing decisions.

Fair Youth: Emylee of Forest Springs marks the first volume in an exciting new book series.

FUTURE PRESIDENTS CLUB
Girls Rule!

Ashley Moore wants to know why there's never been a girl president. Before long the inspired six-year-old creates a special, girls-only club - the **Future Presidents Club**. Meet five enthusiastic young girls who are ready to change the world. ***Future Presidents Club: Girls Rule*** is the first book in a series about girls making a difference!

PRINCESS DESSABELLE
Makes a Friend

Meet **Princess Dessabelle**, a spoiled, lonely princess with a quick temper.

In *Princess Dessabelle Makes a Friend,* the lonely youngster discovers the meaning of true friendship. *Princess Dessabelle: Tennis Star* finds the pampered girl learning the importance of good sportsmanship.

QUINN THE BALLERINA
The Sleeping Beauty!

Quinn the Ballerina can hardly believe it's finally performance day. She's playing her first principal role in a production of *The Sleeping Beauty*.

Yet, Quinn is also nervous. Can she really dance the challenging steps? Will people believe her as a cursed princess caught in a 100-year spell?

Join Quinn as she transforms into Princess Aurora in an exciting retelling of Tchaikovsky's *The Sleeping Beauty*. Now you can relive, or experience for the first time, one of ballet's most acclaimed works as interpreted by a 9 year old.

MAGICAL REBOOTS
Rapunzel

From the popular new series, ***Classical Reboots,*** *Rapunzel* updates the **Brothers Grimm** fairy tale with hilarious and heartbreaking results.

Rapunzel has been locked in her adoptive mother's attic for years. Just as the despondent teenager abandons hope of escaping her private prison, a mysterious tablet computer appears. Before long, Rapunzel's quirky fairy godmother, Aiko, has the conflicted young girl questioning her place in the world.

www.ingramcontent.com/pod-product-compliance
Lightning Source LLC
Chambersburg PA
CBHW071641040426
42452CB00009B/1720